THE MAGIC LADDER TO SUCCESS

THE MAGIC LADDER TO SUCCESS

by Napoleon Hill

Your Step-by-Step Plan to Wealth and Winning from the Author of Think and Grow Rich

Abridged and Introduced
by Mitch Horowitz

THE CONDENSED CLASSICS LIBRARY™

MEDIA

Published by Gildan Media LLC
aka G&D Media.
www.GandDmedia.com

The Magic Ladder to Success was originally published in 1930
G&D Media Condensed Classics edition published 2018
Abridgement and Introduction copyright © 2018 by Mitch
Horowitz

FIRST PRINT AND EBOOK EDITION: 2018

Cover design by David Rheinhardt of Pyrographx

Interior design by Meghan Day Healey of Story Horse, LLC.

ISBN: 978-1-7225-0069-6

Contents

The Birth of a Brave Book

This book began in the mind of one of Napoleon Hill's students. After the 1928 publication of Hill's sixteen-volume *Law of Success*, the writer made a practice of holding "interviews," or what we today would call creativity sessions, with individual students.

One student proved particularly insightful. "Within fifteen minutes after her arrival at the author's office," he wrote, "she had 'stepped up' the vibrations of her mind to where she was 'tuning in' on the Master Mind principles." As a result, Hill continued, a wave of ideas began to "flash" into the student's mind. He wrote down forty of them, the first of which was: "Rewrite the Law of Success philosophy in a brief form which can be presented in one volume, at a very low cost, so it can be placed in the hands of hundreds of thousands of students who might otherwise never have the benefit of such a philosophy of success." Hill's *Magic Ladder to Success*, published in 1930, became that volume.

This Condensed Classics edition further reduces the master's original work to its essentials, so that its full range of seventeen principles are available to you in a single sitting. I have endeavored to preserve every core idea of the original, so that this work comes to you not only with brevity, but also without compromise. It is a working guide to Hill's broadest range of ideas.

One of the benefits of *The Magic Ladder to Success*—and one of the elements I have preserved in this abridgement—is that Hill writes boldly on his theory of how to use "sex energy" as a force for creativity and success. In all of his books, Hill makes the sometimes enigmatic point that the sexual urge is, in fact, the sensation of life's creative force flowing through the individual, and that if this urge, while still being respected on its physical terms, can be channeled *in the direction of achievement*, it may result in works of excellence and even genius. In brief, this technique requires *substituting* another aim or desire for the object of one's sexual urge—and then allowing your creative energies to channel in that direction. Again, Hill does not mean stifling or denying physical sexuality. Not at all. In fact, he underscores the therapeutic value of sexual contact. But rather, Hill induces the reader to become a kind of alchemist who understands redirecting intimate forces for both mental and outer ends.

Hill shrewdly notes that the motive of sexual expression is perhaps the strongest of all motives, since sexuality is the impulse of life replicating itself. He observes that some people have arrived at great inventions, accomplishments, or business successes with the covert intention, unknown perhaps even to themselves, of wooing or pleasing a partner. This brief volume provides sufficient instruction so that you can experiment with these principles on your own.

The Magic Ladder to Success, in this condensation, is probably the briefest but also the most complete digest of Hill's full range of ideas. It is a wonderful entry point for newcomers and a refresher for veterans. It also provides a sense of the broadness of Hill's overall vision. May this book ignite some of your highest efforts and ideas.

—Mitch Horowitz

How to Read
this Book for Profit

For almost a quarter century, I have been writing this book.

The task could not have been completed in less time for several reasons, not the least of which is that I had to inform myself, through years of research, what others had discovered in connection with the causes of failure and success.

Another important reason why my labors have covered nearly a quarter of a century is that I felt it necessary to prove that I could make the Law of Success philosophy work for myself before offering it to others.

I was born in the mountains of the South, in the midst of poverty and illiteracy. For three generations preceding me, my ancestors, on both sides of the house, were content to live in poverty and ignorance, and I would have followed in their footsteps had not my step-mother planted in my mind *the seed of desire* to whip poverty and illiteracy.

From her I got my first impression of the value of a *definite major aim*, and later that impression became so obviously essential as one of the factors of success that I gave it second place in the list of seventeen principles outlined in this book. Except for her influence in plant-ing the seed of ambition in my mind, I never would have written a philosophy of success.

As you read this book, you will observe, as thou-sands of others have, that ideas will begin to "flash" into you mind. Capture these ideas with the aid of a notebook and pencil as they may lead you to the at-tainment of your coveted goal in life. Many students of this philosophy have created valuable inventions while reading the Law of Success. Clergymen have been in-spired by this philosophy to write sermons that lifted them to great heights of eloquence. The Law of Success philosophy is a mind fertilizer. It will cause the mind to function as a magnet that will attract brilliant ideas.

The value of this book is not in its own pages, but in your own reaction to what you read in it. Any brain that can create new ideas in abundance is capable, also, of organizing great power! The main purpose of the Law of Success philosophy is to stimulate the *imagina-*

tive faculties of the brain so they will readily create new and usable ideas for any emergency in life.

Read or listen to this book with pencil in hand, and as you do, note all statements that cause new ideas to "flash" into your mind. This method will serve to fix such ideas in your mind permanently. You cannot assimilate the entire subject matter of this philosophy at one reading or listening of this book. Read or listen to it many times, and each time follow the habit of marking the lines or making notes when you reach passages that inspire new ideas.

This procedure reveals one of the great mysteries of the human mind by introducing you to a source of knowledge that cannot be described adequately to any except those who have discovered this source for themselves. *In this statement lies a hint of the nature of the secret that the Law of Success philosophy has handed over to so many of its students throughout the world!* No one many ever come into possession of this secret except by the method described here.

Before we enter the experience of this book, let us first define success as:

> *The* power *with which to acquire whatever one wants without violating the rights of others.*

The factors through which power may be acquired and used in harmony with this definition number seventeen:

1. The Master Mind
2. A Definite Chief Aim
3. Self-Confidence
4. The Habit of Saving
5. Imagination
6. Initiative and Leadership
7. Enthusiasm
8. Self-Control
9. Doing More Than Paid For
10. A Pleasing Personality
11. Accurate Thinking
12. Cooperation
13. Concentration
14. Profiting by Failures
15. Tolerance
16. The Golden Rule
17. The Habit of Health

The purpose of this book is to *describe* how to apply these seventeen factors so as to acquire personal power for use in any calling and for the solution of one's economic problems. We now turn to an analysis of each factor.

LESSON ONE

The Master Mind

The Master Mind may be defined as: "a composite mind, consisting of two or more individual minds working in perfect harmony, with a definite aim in view."

Recall the definition of success, which is attainable through the application of power, and you will more quickly grasp the meaning of the term Master Mind, as it will be immediately obvious that a group of two or more minds, working in harmony and perfect coordination, will create power in abundance.

All success is achieved through the application of *power.* The staring point, however, may be described as a *burning desire* for the achievement of some specific, definite objective.

Just as the oak tree, in the embryo, sleeps within the acorn, success begins in the form of an intense *desire.* Out of strong desires grow the motivating forces that cause men to cherish hopes, build plans, develop courage, and stimulate their minds to a highly intensified degree of *action* in pursuit of some *definite* plan or purpose.

Desire, then, is the starting point of all human achievement. There is nothing back of desire except the stimuli through which *strong desire* is fanned into a hot flame of *action*. These stimuli are known and have been included as a part of the Law of Success philosophy described in this book.

It has been said, and not without reason, that one may have anything one wants, within reasonable limitations, providing *one wants it badly enough!* Anyone who is capable of stimulating the mind to an intense state of *desire* is capable also of more than average achievement in pursuit of that desire. It must be remembered that wishing for a thing is not the same as *desiring* it with such intensity that out of this desire grow impelling forces of action that drive one to build plans and put those plans to work. A wish is merely a passive form of desire. Most people never advance beyond the wishing stage.

THE BASIC MOTIVATING FORCES OF HUMAN ACTION

There are eight basic motivating forces, one or more of which is the starting point of all noteworthy human achievement. These motivating forces are:

1. The urge of self-preservation
2. The desire for sexual contact
3. The desire for financial gain
4. The desire for life after death
5. The death for fame; to possess *power*
6. The urge of *love* (separate and distinct from the sex urge)
8. The desire for revenge (prevalent in the more undeveloped minds)
9. The desire to indulge one's egotism

Men make use of great power only when urged by one or more of these eight basic motives. The imaginative forces of the human mind become active only when spurred on by the stimulation of a well-defined *motive*! Master salesmen have discovered that all salesmanship is based upon an appeal to one or more of these eight basic motives, which impel men and women to action. Without this discovery no one could become a master salesman.

The Master Mind principle described in this lesson is the medium through which all personal power is applied. For this reason, every known mind stimulant, and every basic motive that inspires action in all human endeavor, are mentioned in this book and chapter.

A Master Mind may be created by any group of people who coordinate their minds in a spirit of perfect harmony. The group may consist of any number from two upward. Best results appear available from the blending of six or seven minds.

It has been suggested that Jesus discovered how to make use of the principle of mind chemistry, and that His seemingly miraculous performances grew out of the power He developed through the blending of the minds of his twelve disciples. It has been pointed out that when one of the disciples, Judas, broke faith, the Master Mind immediately disintegrated and Jesus met with the supreme catastrophe of His life.

When two or more people harmonize their minds and produce the effect known as a Master Mind each person in the group becomes vested with the power to connect with and gather knowledge through the subconscious minds of all the other members. This power becomes immediately noticeable, having the effect of stimulating the mind to a higher rate of vibration, and otherwise evidencing itself in the form of a more vivid imagination and the consciousness of what appears a sixth sense. It is through this sixth sense that new ideas "flash" into the mind. These ideas take on the nature and form of the subject dominating the mind of the individual.

Every public speaker has felt the influence of mind chemistry, for it is well-known that as soon as the individual minds of an audience become en rapport with the speaker (that is, attached to the rate of vibration of the mind of the speaker), there is a noticeable increase of enthusiasm in the speaker's mind, and he often rises to heights of oratory that surprise all, including himself.

It must not be presumed that a Master Mind will immediately spring, mushroom fashion, out of every group of minds that make a pretense of coordination in a spirit of *harmony*! Harmony, in the real sense of the word, is as rare among groups of people as is genuine Christianity among those who proclaim themselves Christian.

Harmony is the nucleus around which the state of mind known as the Master Mind must be developed. Without this element of harmony, there can be no Master Mind, a truth that cannot be repeated too often.

THE RELATIONSHIP BETWEEN SEXUAL URGE AND GENIUS

The urge of sex is, by far, the most powerful of the eight basic motivating factors that stimulate the mind to *action*. Because of the importance of this subject, it has been reserved as the closing segment of the first of the seventeen factors constituting the Law of Success. It is also revisited in the lessons on enthusiasm and the habit of health.

The part that the sexual urge plays in the achievement of outstanding success was first discovered by the author in his studies of the biographies of great leaders, and in his analysis of men and women of the present age who have risen high in their fields. But to be highly sexed is not sufficient, of itself, to produce a genius. Only those who understand the nature of sexual urge, and who know how to *transmute* this powerful emotion into other channels of action than that of sexual contact, rise to the status of a genius. The urge of sex is a driving force compared to which all other motives must take second place. A mind that has been aroused through intense sexual desire becomes receptive to that impulse of ideas that "flash" into the mind from outside sources through what is ordinarily known as "inspiration."

It is the belief of this author—a belief not without considerable evidence to back it—that all so-called "revelations," of whatever nature, from religion to art, are super-induced by intense desire for sexual contact. All so-called "magnetic" people are highly sexed. People who are brilliant, charming, versatile, and accomplished are generally high sexed. Prove this for yourself by analyzing those whom you know to be highly sexed.

It is a fact well known to scientists, although not generally known to the layman, that sexual contact has a therapeutic value unknown in connection with any other human emotion. This fact may be easily verified, however, by even the most casual study of the subject, by observing the physical state of the body following sexual contact between two people who are properly mated or affinitized. What mind is so vulgar and ignorant as not to have observed that following sexual contact, between two people who are properly "balanced," or mated, the physical body becomes relaxed or calm? Relaxation, super-induced in this manner, provides the nervous system with a favorable opportunity to balance and distribute the nervous energy of the body to all of its organs.

A great, enduring love is a sufficient motive to drive even a mediocre man to unbelievable heights of achievement, a statement of fact that should be kept in mind by all spouses.

In short, *sexual urge is the most effective known agency through which the mind may be "stepped up" to where it becomes a Master Mind!*

THE TEN MAJOR SOURCES OF MIND STIMULATION

It may be helpful here to outline the major sources of mind stimulation, in view of the fact that all great achievements result from some form of stimuli that "step up" the mind to a high rate of vibration. These stimuli are listed in the order of what the author considers their importance:

1. *Sexual contact* between two people who are motivated by a genuine feeling of love.
2. *Love* not necessarily accompanied by sexual contact.
3. *Burning desire* for fame, power, and financial gain.
4. *Music,* which acts as a mighty stimulant to a highly emotionalized person.
5. *Friendship,* between either those of the same sex or the opposite sex, accompanied by a desire to be mutually helpful in some definite undertaking.
6. *Master Mind alliance,* between two or more people who ally themselves, mentally, for the purpose of mutual help, in a spirit of unselfishness.
7. *Mutual suffering,* such as that experienced by people who are unjustly persecuted, for reasons of race, religion, or economics.
8. *Autosuggestion,* through which an individual may step up his or her own mind, through constant self-suggestion with a definite motive.
9. *Suggestion.* The influence of *outside* suggestion may lift one to great heights of achievement, or, if negatively used, dash one to the pit of failure and destruction.
10. *Narcotics and alcohol.* This source of mind stimulation is totally destructive, and leads, finally, to negation of all the other nine sources of stimulation.

Through these sources of stimulation one may commune, temporarily, with Infinite Intelligence, a procedure that constitutes all there is of genius. *The foregoing statement is definite and plain. Take it or leave it, just as you please!* The statement is made as a positive fact because this author has had the privilege of helping to raise scores of mediocre men and women out of mediocrity into states of mind that entitled them to rank as geniuses. Some have been able to remain in this exalted state, while others have relapsed to their former status, either temporarily or permanently.

Again, the desire for sexual contact is the strongest, most powerful, and most impelling of all human desires, and for this very reason it may be harnessed and transmuted into channels other than that of sexual contact in a manner that will raise one to great heights of genius. On the other hand, this powerful urge, if not controlled and so transmuted, may and often does lower man to the level of an ordinary beast.

A Definite Chief Aim

To be successful in any sort of endeavor you must have a *definite* goal toward which to work. You must have definite plans for attaining this goal. Nothing worthwhile is ever accomplished without a definite plan that is systematically and continuously followed out day by day.

A *definite chief aim* is placed at the beginning of the Seventeen Laws of Success for the reason that without it the other Sixteen Laws would be useless, for how could one know when he had succeeded, without first having determined what he wanted to accomplish?

Careful study of more than one hundred of the leading men in practically all walks of life has disclosed that every one of these men worked with a *definite chief aim* and also a *definite plan* for its attainment.

The human mind is something like a magnet in that it will attract the counterparts of the dominating thoughts held in the mind, and especially those that constitute a *definite chief aim* or purpose. For example, if a man establishes, as his *definite chief aim*, and as his daily working purpose, the adding of, say, one hundred new customers who will regularly purchase the merchandise or service he is rendering, immediately that aim or purpose becomes a dominating influence in his mind, and this influence will drive him to do whatever is necessary to secure these additional one hundred customers.

Your first step on the road to success is to know where you are going, how you intend to travel, and when you intend to get there, which is only another way of saying that you must determine a *definite chief aim*. This aim, when decided upon, must be written out in clear language, so it can be understood by any other person. If there is anything "hazy" about your aim, it is not *definite*. A man who knew what he was saying once stated that nine-tenths of success, in any undertaking, is in knowing *what is wanted*. This is true.

The moment you write out a statement of your *chief aim*, your action plants an image of that aim firmly in your subconscious mind. Nature causes your subconscious mind to use that chief aim as a pattern or blueprint by which the major portion of your thoughts, ideas, and efforts are directed toward the attainment of the objective on which the *aim* is based.

This is a strange, abstract truth—something that cannot be weighed, meditated upon—but is a truth nevertheless!

Self-Confidence

The third of the Seventeen Laws of Success is self-confidence. The term is self-explanatory—it means that to achieve success you must believe in yourself. However, this does not mean that you have no limitations; it means that you are to take inventory of yourself, find out what qualities you have that are strong and useful, and then organize these qualities into a *definite plan* of action with which to attain the object of your *definite chief aim*.

In all the languages of the world there is no one word that carries the same or even approximately the same meaning as *"faith."* If there are any such things as "miracles," they are performed only with the aid of super-faith. The doubting type of mind is not a creative mind. Search where and how you may, and you will not discover a single record of great achievement in any line of endeavor that was not conceived in the imagination and brought into reality through *faith*!

To succeed, you must have faith in your own ability to do whatever you make up your mind to do. Also, you must cultivate the habit of faith in those who are associated with you, whether they are in a position of authority over you, or you over them. The psychological reason for this will be covered later in the law of cooperation.

A *definite chief aim* is the starting point of all noteworthy achievement, but self-confidence is the unseen force that coaxes, drives, or leads one on and on until the object of the aim is a reality. Many people have vague sorts of aims, but they get nowhere because they lack the self-confidence to create *definite plans* for attaining these aims.

Fear is the main enemy of self-confidence. Every person comes into the world cursed, to some extent, with Six Basic Fears, all of which must be mastered before one may develop sufficient self-confidence to attain outstanding success.

The six basic fears are:

1. The Fear of Criticism
2. The Fear of Ill Health
3. The Fear of Poverty
4. The Fear of Old Age

5. The Fear of Loss of Love (ordinarily called jealousy)
6. The Fear of Death

Space will not permit a lengthy description of how and where these Six Fears came from. In the main, however, they were acquired through early childhood environment. Fear of Criticism is placed at the head of the list because it is, perhaps, the most common and one of the most destructive of the entire six fears.

Before you can develop self-confidence sufficient to master the obstacles that stand between you and success, you must take inventory of yourself and find out how many of these six basic fears are standing in your way. A few days of study, thought, and reflection will enable you to lay your fingers on the particular fear or fears that stand between you and self-confidence.

The Habit of Saving

I t is an embarrassing admission, but true, that a poverty-stricken person is less than the dust of the earth as far as the achievement of noteworthy success is concerned. It may be, and perhaps is true, that *money is not success*. But unless you have it or can command its use, you will not get far, no matter what may be your *definite chief aim*. As business is conducted today—as civilization stands to today—money is an absolute essential for success, and there is no known formula for financial independence except that which is connected, in one way or another, with systematic saving.

The amount saved from week to week or from month to month is not of great consequence so long as the saving is regular and systematic. This is true because the habit of saving adds something to the other qualities essential for success, which can be had in no other way.

It is doubtful if any person can develop self-confidence to the highest possible point without the protection and independence that belong to those who have saved and are saving money. There is something about the knowledge that one has some money ahead that gives faith and self-reliance such as can be had no other way.

Without money, a person is at the mercy of everyone who wishes to exploit or prey upon him. If the man who does not save and has no money offers his personal services for sale, he must accept whatever the purchaser offers; there is no alternative.

If opportunity to profit by trade, or otherwise, comes along it is of no avail to the man who has neither money nor credit, and it must be kept in mind that credit is generally based upon the money one has or its equivalent.

The amount of your income is of little importance if you do not systematically save a portion of it.

Railroad magnate James J. Hill once named a rule by which any man may test himself and determine, well in advance, whether he will succeed in life. That rule is: "He must have formed the habit of systematic saving of money."

Initiative and Leadership

All people may be placed in one or the other of two general classes. One is known as leaders and the other as followers. The followers rarely achieve noteworthy success, and never succeed until they break away from the ranks of followers and become leaders.

There is a mistaken notion broadcast in the world to the effect that a man is paid for what he knows. This is only partly true, and like all other half-truths, it does more damage than an outright falsehood.

The truth is, a man is paid not only for what he *knows*, but more particularly for what *he does* with what he knows, or that which he *gets others to do*.

Without *initiative* no man will achieve success, no matter what he may consider success, because he will do nothing out of the ordinary run of mediocre work such as nearly all men are forced to do in order have a place to sleep, something to eat, and clothes to wear. These three necessities may be had, of a certain kind, without the aid of *initiative* and *leadership*, but the moment a man makes up his mind to acquire more than the bare necessities of life, he must either cultivate the habits of *initiative* and *leadership* or else find himself hedged in behind a stone wall.

The first step essential to the development of *initiative* and *leadership* is that of forming the habit of prompt and firm *decision*. All successful people have a certain amount of *decision*. The man who wavers between two or more half-baked and more or less vague notions of what he wants to do generally ends by doing nothing.

It is not enough to have a *definite chief aim* and a *definite plan* for its attainment, even though the plan may be perfectly practical and you may have all the necessary ability to carry it through successfully. You must have more than these. You must actually take the *initiative* and put the wheels of your plan into motion and keep them turning until your goal is reached.

Study those whom you know to be failures (you'll find them all around you) and observe that, without a single exception, they lack firmness of *decision,* even in matters of the smallest importance. Such people usually talk a great deal, but they are very short on performance. "Deeds, not words," should be the motto of anyone who intends to succeed in life, no matter what may be his calling, or what he has selected as his *definite chief aim.*

Imagination

No man ever accomplished anything, never created anything, never built any plan or developed a *definite chief aim* without the use of his *imagination*.

Everything that any man ever created or built was first visioned, in his own mind, through *imagination*.

In the workshop of the *imagination* one may take old, well-known ideas or concepts, or parts of ideas, and combine them with still other old ideas or parts of ideas, and out of this combination create what seems to be new. This process is the major principle of all invention.

One may have a *definite chief aim* and a plan for achieving it; may possess *self-confidence*; may have a highly developed *habit of saving*; and possess both *initiative* and *leadership* in abundance—but if the element of imagination is missing, these other qualities will be useless because there will be no driving force to shape their use.

Thomas Edison developed the electric bulb by use of his *imagination* when he assembled two old and well-known principles in a combination in which they had never before been associated. A brief description of just how this was accomplished will help you to vision the manner in which *imagination* may be made to solve problems, overcome obstacles, and the lay foundation for great achievements.

Edison discovered, as others had before him, that a light could be created by applying electrical energy to a wire, thus heating the wire to a white heat. The trouble, however, came because no one had found a way to control the heat. The wire soon burned out when heated sufficiently to give a clear light.

After many years of experimentation, Edison happened to think of the old, well-known method of burning charcoal, and saw, instantly, that this principle held the secret to the needed control of heat essential in creating a light by applying electrical power to a wire.

Charcoal is made by placing a pile of wood on the ground, setting the wood on fire, and then covering it over with dirt, thereby cutting off most of the oxygen from the fire, which enables the wood to burn slowly; but it cannot blaze and the stick cannot burn up entirely. This is because there can be no combustion where there is no oxygen, and little combustion where there is little oxygen. With this knowledge in mind, Edison went into his laboratory, placed the wire with which he had been experimenting inside a vacuum tube, thus cutting off *all* the oxygen, applied the electrical power, and lo! he had a perfect incandescent light bulb. The wire inside the bulb could not burn up because there was no oxygen inside to create combustion sufficient to burn it up.

So it happened that one of the most useful modern inventions was created by combining two principles in a new way.

There is nothing absolutely new!

That which seems new is but a combination of ideas or elements of something old. This is literally true in the creation of business plans, inventions, the manufacture of metals, and everything else created by man.

To cultivate the *imagination* so it will eventually suggest ideas on its own initiative, you should make it your business to keep a record of all the useful, ingenious, and practical ideas you see in use in other lines of work outside your own, as well as in connection with your work. Start with an ordinary pocket-sized notebook, and catalogue every idea, concept, or thought that occurs to you, which is capable of practical use, and then take these ideas and work them into new plans. By and by, the time will come when the powers of your own *imagination* will go into the storehouse of your own subconscious mind, where all the knowledge that you have ever gathered is stored, assemble this knowledge into new combinations, and hand over to you the results in the shape of *new ideas*, or what appear to be new ideas.

This procedure is practical because it has been followed successfully by some of the best-known leaders, investors, and businessmen.

Let us here define the word *imagination* as: "The workshop of the mind wherein may be assembled, in new and varying combinations, all ideas, thoughts, plans, facts, theories, and principles known to man."

A single combination of ideas, which may be merely parts of old and well-known ideas, may be worth anywhere from a few cents to a few million dollars.

The dreamer who does nothing more than dream uses the imagination, but he falls short of using this great faculty efficiently because he does not add to it the impulse to put his thoughts into *action*. Here is where *initiative* enters and goes to work for him, providing he is familiar with the Laws of Success and understands that ideas, of themselves, are worthless until put into action.

The dreamer who creates practical ideas must place back of these ideas three of the laws that have preceded this one, namely:

1. The Law of a Definite Chief Aim
2. The Law of Self-Confidence
3. The Law of Initiative and Leadership

Enthusiasm

It seems more than coincidence that the most successful people, in all walks of life—and particularly in sales—are the enthusiastic type.

Enthusiasm is a driving force that not only gives greater power to the man who has it, but it is contagious and affects all whom it reaches. Enthusiasm over the work in which one is engaged takes the drudgery out of that work. Enthusiasm gives greater power to one's efforts, no matter what sort of work one is in.

The starting point of enthusiasm is "motive," or well-defined desire. Enthusiasm is simply a high rate of vibration of the mind. Elsewhere in this book may be found a complete list of the mind stimulants that will super-induce the state of mind known as enthusiasm. The urge of sexual desire is the greatest-known mind stimulant. People who do not feel a strong desire for sexual contact are seldom, if ever, capable of becoming highly enthusiastic over anything. Transmutation of the great driving force of sex desire is the basis of practically all the works of genius. By "transmutation" is meant the switching of thought from sexual contact to any other form of physical action.

It is a well-known fact that men succeed most readily when engaged in an occupation that they like best, and this for the reason that they readily become enthusiastic over that which they like best. Enthusiasm is also the basis of creative imagination. When the mind is vibrating at a high rate, it is receptive to similarly high rates of vibration, from outside sources, thus providing a favorable condition for creative imagination. It will be observed that enthusiasm plays an important part in four of the other principles constituting the Law of Success philosophy, namely, the Master Mind, Imagination, Accurate Thought, and Pleasing Personality.

Enthusiasm, to be of value, must be controlled and directed to definite ends. Uncontrolled enthusiasm may be, and generally is, destructive. The acts of so-called "bad boys" are generally nothing more than uncontrolled enthusiasm. The wasted energy of uncontrolled enthusiasm expressed through promiscuous sexual contact, and sex desire not expressed through contact, is sufficient to lift one to high achievement if this urge is harnessed and transformed into some other form of physical action.

The next chapter, on self-control, appropriately follows the subject of enthusiasm, since self-control is necessary in the mastery of enthusiasm.

Self-Control

Lack of self-control has brought grief to more people than any other shortcoming known to the human race. This evil shows itself, at one time or another, in everyone's life.

Every successful person must have some sort of a balance wheel for his or her emotions.

The man who lacks self-control may be easily mastered by one who has such control, and tricked into saying or doing that which may later prove embarrassing to him.

Success in life is very largely a matter of harmonious negotiation with other people, and this requires self-control in abundance.

An angry man is suffering from a degree of temporary insanity, and therefore he is hardly capable of diplomatic negotiation with others. For this reason, the angry man, or the one who has no self-control, is an easy victim of the man who has such control. No man may become powerful without first gaining control of himself.

Self-control is also a balance wheel for the person who is too optimistic and whose enthusiasm needs checking, for it is possible to become entirely too enthusiastic; so much so that one becomes a bore to all those near him.

Habit of Doing More Than Paid For

This law has proven a stumbling block to many promising careers. There is a general attitude among people to perform as little service as they can get by with; but if you study these people carefully, you will observe that while they may be actually "getting by" temporarily, they are not, however, getting anything else.

There are two major reasons why all successful people must practice the law of doing more than paid for:

1. Just as an arm or limb grows strong through use, so does the mind grow strong. By rendering the greatest possible amount of service, the faculties through which the service is rendered are put into use and, eventually, become strong and accurate.

2. By rendering more service than you are paid for, you will be turning the spotlight of *favorable* attention upon yourself, and it will not be long before you will be sought with fancy offers for your services, and there will be a continuous market for those services.

"Do the thing and you shall have the power," was the admonition of Emerson.

By rendering more service and better service than that for which you are paid, you also take advantage of the Law of Increasing Returns, through the operation of which you will eventually be paid, in one way or another, for far more service than you actually perform.

You will not find many people many rendering such service, which is all the better for you, because you will stand in bold contrast with practically all others who are engaged in a work similar to yours. *Contrast* is a powerful law, and you may, in this manner, profit by it.

If the author had to choose one of the seventeen laws of success as the most important, and had to discard all the others except the one chosen, he would, without a moment's hesitation, chose this Law of *Rendering More Service and Better Service than Paid for.*

Pleasing Personality

A pleasing personality, naturally, is one that does not antagonize. Personality cannot be defined in one word, nor in half a dozen words, for it represents the sum total of all one's characteristics, good and bad.

Your personality is totally unlike any other personality. It is the sum of qualities, emotions, characteristics, appearances, etc., which distinguish you from all other people.

Your clothes form an important part of your personality; the way you wear them, the harmony of colors you select, the quality, and many other details all go to indicate much that belongs distinctly as a part of your personality. Some psychologists claim that they can accurately analyze any person, in many important respects, by turning that person loose in a clothing store where there is a great variety of clothing, with instructions to select whatever may be wanted and dress in the clothes selected.

Your facial expression, as shown by the lines of your face, or the lack of lines, forms an important part of your personality. Your voice, its pitch, tone, volume, and the language you use form important parts of your personality because they mark you instantly, once you have spoken, as a person of refinement or the opposite.

The manner in which you shake hands constitutes an important part of your personality. If, when shaking hands, you merely hold out a cold hunk of flesh and bones that is limp and lifeless, you are displaying a sign of a personality that is not mixed with *enthusiasm* or *initiative.*

A pleasing personality is usually found in one who speaks gently and kindly, selecting refined words that do not offend, in a modest tone of voice; who selects clothing of appropriate style and colors, which harmonize; who is unselfish and not only willing, but desirous, of serving others; who is a friend of all humanity, rich and the poor alike, regardless of politics, religion or occupation; who refrains from speaking unkindly of others, either with or without cause; who manages to converse without being drawn into vulgar conversations or useless arguments on such debatable topics as religion and politics; who sees both good and bad in people, but makes due allowance for the latter; who seeks neither to reform nor to reprimand others; who smiles frequently and deeply; who loves music and little children; who sympathizes with all who are in trouble and forgives acts of unkindness; who willingly grants others the right to do as they please as long as no one's rights are interfered with; who earnestly strives to be constructive in every thought and deed indulged in; who encourages others and spurs them on to greater and better achievement.

Life may be properly called a great drama in which good showmanship is of the utmost importance. Successful people, in all callings, are generally good showmen; meaning, by this, that they practice the habit of catering or playing to the crowd.

A good showman is one who understands how to cater to the masses. Success is not a matter of chance or luck. It is the result of careful planning, careful staging, and able acting of parts by the player in the game.

What is to be done about this defect by the man who is not blessed with a personality that lends itself to able showmanship? Is such a person to be doomed to failure because of Nature's oversight in not blessing him with such a personality?

Not at all. Here is where the principle of the Master Mind comes to the rescue. Those who do not have pleasing personalities may surround themselves with men and women who supply this defect. Henry Ford was not blessed, by Nature, with native ability as a good showman, and his personality was not perfect by a long way, but, knowing how to make use of the Master Mind Principle, he bridged this defect by surrounding himself with men who did have such ability.

What are the most essential characteristics of good showmanship?

First, the ability to appeal to the imagination of the public, and to keep people interested and curious concerning one's activities. Second, a keen sense of appreciation of the value of psychological appeal through advertising. Third, sufficient alertness of mind to enable one to capture and make use of the prejudices, likes, and dislikes of the public, at the psychological moment.

Accurate Thinking

The art of accurate thinking is not difficult to acquire, although certain definite rules must be followed. To think accurately, one must follow at least two basic principles:

1. Accurate thinking calls for the separation of *facts* from mere *information*.
2. *Facts*, when ascertained, must be separated into two classes; one is known as *important* and the other as *unimportant*, or irrelevant.

The question naturally arises, "What is an *important fact?*" and the answer is: An *important fact* is essential for the attainment of one's *definite chief aim* or purpose, or which may be useful or necessary in connection with one's daily occupation. All other facts, while they may be useful and interesting, are comparatively unimportant as far as the individual is concerned.

No one has the right to an opinion on any subject, unless he has arrived at that opinion by a process of reasoning based upon all the available *facts* connected with the subject. Despite this, however, nearly everyone has opinions on nearly every subject, whether they are familiar with those subjects, or have any *facts* connected with them or not.

Be careful, also, that you do not indulge in wild, speculative language that is not based upon *known facts*.

It often requires considerable effort to *know facts* on any subject, which is perhaps \ why so few people take the time or go to the trouble to gather *facts* as the basis of their opinions.

You are presumably following this philosophy for the purpose of learning how you may become more successful; and if that is true then *you* must break away from the common practices of the masses who do not think and take the time to gather facts as the basis of thought. That this requires effort is freely admitted, but it must be kept in mind that *success* is not something that one may pluck from a tree, where it has grown of its own accord. Success is something that represents perseverance, self-sacrifice, determination, and strong character.

Everything has its price, and nothing may be obtained without paying the price; or, if something of value is obtained, it cannot be retained for long. The price of accurate thought is the effort required to gather and organize the *facts* on which to base the *thought*.

Concentration

The jack-of-all-trades seldom accomplishes much at any trade. Life is so complex, and there are so many ways of dissipating energy unprofitably, that the habit of *concentrated effort* must be formed and adhered to by all who succeed.

Power is based upon organized effort or energy. Energy cannot be organized without the habit of *concentration* of all the faculties on one thing at a time. An ordinary reading glass may be used to so focus the rays of the sun that they will burn a hole in a board in a few minutes. Those same rays will not even heat the board until they are *concentrated* on one spot.

The human mind is something like the reading glass, because it is the medium through which all the faculties of the brain may be brought together and made to function in a coordinated fashion. It is worthy of serious consideration to remember that all the outstanding men of success, in all walks of life, concentrated the major portion of their thoughts and efforts upon one *definite purpose, objective,* or *chief aim.*

Find out what you wish to do—adopt a *definite chief aim*—then concentrate all your energies back of this purpose until it has reached a happy climax.

Observe, in analyzing the next law, on *cooperation,* the close connection between the principles outlined and those associated with the law of *concentration.*

Wherever a group of people ally themselves in an organized, cooperative spirit for the carrying out of some definite purpose, it will be observed that they are employing the law of *concentration,* and unless they do so their alliance will be without real power.

Cooperation

We are living distinctly in an age of *cooperation*. The outstanding achievements in business, industry, finance, transportation, and politics are all based upon the principle of cooperative effort.

To succeed in a big way, in any undertaking, means that one must have the cooperation of others. The winning football team is the one that is best coached in the art of *cooperation*. The spirit of teamwork must prevail in business, or the business will not get very far.

You will observe that some of the preceding laws must be practiced as a matter of habit before you can get perfect cooperation from others. For example, other people will not cooperate with you unless you have mastered and applied the law of a *pleasing personality*. You will also notice that *enthusiasm* and *self-control* and the *habit of doing more than paid for* must be practiced before you hope to gain the full cooperation from others.

These laws overlap one another, and all of them must be merged into the law of *cooperation*, which means that one, to gain cooperation from others, must form the habit of practicing the laws named.

No man is willing to cooperate with a person who has an offensive personality. No man is willing to cooperate with one who is not enthusiastic, or who lacks self-control. *Power* comes from organized, *cooperative* effort!

A dozen well-trained soldiers, working with perfectly coordinated effort, can master a mob of a thousand people who lack leadership and organization.

You may test this out, in your own way, by watching the reaction of your own mind when you are in the presence of those with whom you are friendly compared with what happens when you are in the presence of those who you do not like. Friendly association inspires one with a mysterious energy not otherwise experienced, and this great truth is the foundation stone of the law of *cooperation*.

An army that is forced to fight because the soldiers are afraid they will be shot down by their own leaders may be a very effective army, but such an army never has been a match for an army that goes into action of its own accord, with every man determined to win because he believes his side ought to win.

Profiting By Failure

Failure is one of the most beneficial parts of a human being's experience, for the reason that there are many needed lessons that must be learned before one commences to succeed, which could be learned from no teacher other than *failure*.

Failure is a blessing in disguise providing it teaches us some useful lesson that we could not or would not have learned without it!

However, millions of people make the mistake of accepting *failure* as final, whereas it is, like most other events in life, but transitory, and for this reason should not be accepted as final.

Successful people must learn to distinguish between failure and *temporary defeat*. Every person experiences, at one time or another, some form of temporary defeat, and out of such experiences come some of the greatest and most beneficial lessons.

In truth, most of us are so constituted that if we never experienced temporary defeat (or what some ignorantly call *failure*), we would soon become so egotistical and independent that we would imagine ourselves more important than Deity.

Headaches are beneficial, despite the fact that they are very disagreeable, because they represent Nature's language in which she calls loudly for intelligent use of the body.

It is the same regarding temporary defeat or failure—these are Nature's symbols through which she signals us that we have been headed in the wrong direction, and if we are reasonably intelligent we heed these signals, steer a different course, and come, finally to the objective of our *definite chief aim*.

One of the most starting discoveries in my research was that all outstanding successes, regardless of the field in which they were engaged, were people who met with reverses, adversity, temporary defeat, and, in some instances, actual *permanent failure* (as far as they, as individuals, were concerned). Not a single successful person was discovered whose success was attained without the experience of what, in many instances, seemed like unbearable obstacles, which had to be mastered.

It was discovered also that in exact ratio to the extent that these successful people met squarely and did not budge from defeat that they arose to the heights of success. In other words, success is measured, always, by the extent to which any individual meets and squarely deals with the obstacles that arise in the course of this procedure in pursuit of his *definite chief aim*.

Do not be afraid of temporary defeat, but make sure that you learn some lesson from every such defeat. That which we call "experience" consists, largely, of what we learn by mistakes—our own and those made by others—but we cannot ignore the knowledge that may be gained from mistakes.

Tolerance

Intolerance has caused more grief than any other of man's many forms of ignorance.

It is impossible for any man to observe the law of *accurate thought* without having first acquitted the habit of tolerance, for the reason that intolerance causes a man to slam shut the Book of Knowledge and write on its cover, "Finis, I know it all!"

Intolerance is closely related to *the six basic fears* described in the law of *self-confidence,* and it may be stated as a positive fact that intolerance is always the result of either *fear* or *ignorance.* There are no exceptions to this. The moment another person (providing he, himself, is not intolerant) discovers that you are cursed with intolerance he can easily and quickly mark you as being either the victim of *fear* and *superstition,* or, what's worse, ignorance.

Intolerance closes the doorway to opportunity in a thousand ways, and shuts out the light of intelligence.

The moment you open your mind to *facts*, and take the attitude that the last word is seldom said on any subject—that there always remains the chance that still more truth may be learned on every subject—you begin to cultivate the law of *tolerance*, and if you practice this habit for long you will soon become a thinker, with ability to solve the problems that confront you in your struggle to make a place for yourself in your chosen field.

Practicing the Golden Rule

This is, in some ways, the most important of the Seventeen Laws of Success. Despite the fact that the great philosophers for more than five thousand years have all discovered the law of the Golden Rule, and have made comment on it, the great majority of people today look upon it as a sort of pretty text for preachers to build sermons on.

In truth, the Golden Rule is based upon a powerful law that, when understood and faithfully practiced, will enable any man to get others to *cooperate* with him.

It is a well-known truth that most men follow the practice of returning good or evil, act for act. If you slander a man, he will slander you. If you praise a man, he will praise you. If you favor a man in business, he will favor you in return.

There are exceptions to this rule, to be sure, but by and large the law works out. Like attracts like. This is in accordance with a great natural law, and it works in every particle of matter and in every form of energy in the universe. Successful men attract successful men. Failures attract failures.

The law of the Golden Rule is closely related to the law of *the habit of doing more than paid for.* The very act of rendering more service than you are paid for puts into operation this law through which like attracts like, which is the selfsame law as that which forms the basis of the Golden Rule.

This law is so fundamental, so obvious, and so simple. Yet it is one of the great mysteries of human nature that it is not more generally understood and practiced. Back of its use lie possibilities that stagger the imagination of the most visionary person. Through its use one may learn the real secret—all the secret there is—to the art of *getting others to that which we wish them to do.*

If you want a favor from someone, make it your business to seek out the person from whom you want the favor and, in an appropriate manner, render that person an equivalent of the favor you wish from him. If he does not respond at first, double the dose and render him another favor, and another, and another, and so on, until finally he will, out of shame if nothing more, come back and render you a favor.

You get others to cooperate with you by first cooperating with them.

The foregoing sentence is worth reading a hundred times, for it contains the gist of one of the most powerful laws available to the man who has the intention of attaining great success.

It may sometimes happen, and it will, that the particular individual to whom you render useful service will never respond and render you a similar service, but *keep this important truth in mind*—that even though one person fails to respond, someone else will observe the transaction and, out of a sportsman's desire to see justice done, or perhaps with a more selfish motive in mind, will render you the service to which you are entitled.

"Whatsoever a man soweth that shall he also reap."

This is more than mere preachment; it is a great practical truth that may be made the foundation of every successful achievement.

The Habit of Health

We come now to the last of the seventeen factors of success. In previous chapters we learned that success grows out of power; that power is organized knowledge expressed in definite action. No one can remain intensively active very long without good health. The mind will not function properly unless it has a sound body in which to function. Practically all of the other sixteen factors that enter into the building of success depend, for their successful application, upon a healthy body.

As a closing thought for this chapter, the author wishes to return to a very brief statement concerning the therapeutic value of sex energy. The foundation of fact that justifies reference to sex, as a health builder, will be laid out in the following manner:

It is a well-known fact that *thought* is the most powerful energy available to man. It is equally well known that negative thoughts of worry, envy, hatred, and fear will destroy the digestive processes and bring about illness; this is because negative thought inhibits the flow of certain glandular contents that are essential in the digestive processes.

Negative thoughts cause "short circuits" in the nerve lines that carry nervous energy (or life force) from the central distributing station, the brain, to all parts of the body, where this energy performs its natural task of nourishment and of removal of worn out cells and waste matter.

Sex energy is a highly vitalizing, positive force, when it is in a state of agitation, during the period of sexual contact, and because it is powerful it sweeps over the entire nervous system of the body and unties any "short circuits" that may exist in any of the nerve lines, thus ensuring a complete flow of nervous energy to *all* parts of the body.

Sexual emotion is the most powerful of all the human emotions, and when it is actively engaged, it reaches and vitalizes every cell in every organ of the body, thereby causing the organs to function in a normal manner. Total abstinence, sexually, was not one of Nature's plans, and those who do not understand this truth, usually pay for their ignorance out of a trust fund that Nature provided for the maintenance of health.

Thought controls all voluntary movements of the body. Are we in accord on this statement? Very well, if thought controls all voluntary movements of the body, may it also be made to control, or at least materially influence, all involuntary movements of the body?

Thoughts of a negative nature, such as fear, worry, and anxiety, not only inhibit the flow of the digestive juices, but they also "tie knots" in the nerve lines which carry nervous energy to the various organs of the body.

Thoughts of a *positive* nature untie these knots in the nerve lines and permit the nervous energy to pass through. *Sex emotion is the most powerful form of positive thought.* Sex energy is Nature's own "medicine," proof of which is obvious if one will observe the state of mind and the perfectly relaxed condition of the body following sexual contact.

Brief as it is, the foregoing statement should be made the starting point for some intelligent analysis of this subject by the reader of this book. No one knows the last word in connection with the subject; most of us do not even know the first word. Therefore, let us not pass judgment on a subject concerning which we know so very little until we at least have done some intelligent thinking on the subject. For all that most of us know, both poverty and ill health may be mastered through a complete understanding of the subject of sex energy, and for that reason sex energy is the most powerful mind stimulant known.

The Mystery of the Power of Thought

Every man is where he is as the result of his own dominating thoughts, just as surely as night follows day. Thought is the only thing that you absolutely control, a statement of fact that we repeat because it is of great significance. You do not control, entirely, the money you possess, or the love and friendship that you enjoy; you had nothing to do with your coming into the world and you will have little to do with the time of your going; but you can make the mind *positive* or you can permit it to become *negative*, as the result of outside influences and suggestions. Divine Providence gave you supreme control of your own mind, and with this control the responsibility is now yours to make the best use of it.

The difference between success and failure is largely a matter of the difference between positive and negative thought. A negative mind will not attract a fortune. Like attracts like. Nothing attracts success as quickly as success. Poverty begets more poverty. Become successful and the whole world will lay its treasures at your feet and want to do something to help you become more successful. Show signs of poverty and the entire world will try to take away that which you have of value. You can borrow money at the bank when you are prosperous and do not need it, but try and arrange a loan when you are poverty-stricken, or when some great emergency faces you. You are the master of your own destiny because you control the one thing that can change and redirect the course of human destinies, the power of *thought*.

Let this great truth sink into your consciousness and this book will have marked the most important turning point of your life.

ABOUT THE AUTHORS

NAPOLEON HILL was born in 1883 in Wise County, Virginia. He was employed as a secretary, a reporter for a local newspaper, the manager of a coalmine and a lumberyard, and attended law school, before he began working as a journalist for *Bob Taylor's Magazine,* an inspirational and general-interest journal. In 1908, the job led to his interviewing steel magnate Andrew Carnegie. The encounter, Hill said, changed the course of his life. Carnegie believed success could be distilled into principles that anyone could follow, and urged Hill to interview the greatest industrialists, financiers, and inventors of the era to discover these principles. Hill accepted the challenge, which lasted more than twenty years and formed the building block for *Think and Grow Rich.* Hill dedicated the rest of his life to documenting and refining the principles of success. After a long career as an author, magazine publisher, lecturer, and consultant to business leaders, the motivational pioneer died in 1970 in South Carolina.

MITCH HOROWITZ, who abridged and introduced this volume, is the PEN Award-winning author of books including *Occult America* and *The Miracle Club: How Thoughts Become Reality. The Washington Post* says Mitch "treats esoteric ideas and movements with an even-handed intellectual studiousness that is too often lost in today's raised-voice discussions." Follow him @MitchHorowitz.